Acknowledgements:

I would like to take this time to thank everyone that helped me on this project. I would like to thank my wife and kids who inspired me to write this book.

HOW TO BUILD PERSONAL CREDIT MADE EASY

TABLE OF CONTENTS

Why Credit is so important 1

Ways to create and Improve Personal Credit with Tools of Engagement .. 3

    What is Annual Fee? 9

    Six ways to lower your Credit Card Balances 10

    1. Pay down your balance early 10

    2. Decrease your spending. 12

    3. Pay off your credit card balances with a private loan. 12

    4. Increase your credit limit. 13

    5. Open a replacement Credit Card. 13

    6. Don't close unused cards. 14

    What Is a Credit-Builder Loan? 15

    How to manage a credit-builder loan 15

    How does a credit builder loan work 16

How to Apply for a Credit Card 18

    1. Realize credit scores 18

    2. Access your credit scores 18

    3. Improve your credit 19

    4. Don't apply for credit until you understand it 20

    5. Include all income within the application 20

A primary card holder vs. authorized user 21

    What is a primary card holder? 21

    How to become an authorized user. 21

    How to use a Personal Loan to create credit 22

    Late payments will hurt your credit. 23

    Bad-credit and no-credit personal loans are expensive. 23

    Short-term loans are often dangerous. 24

    Not all personal lenders report back to the main credit bureaus 24

How to Report Rent Payments to an agency 24
    a. Check with Your Landlord 25
    b. Use credit cards to pay your rent. 25
    c. Use a Rent Reporting Service 26
    d. Making Rent Payments 27

How to make timely payments on all of your bills 28
    1. Make an inventory of each bill 28
    2. Determine when your payments are due..................................29
    3. Add your payments to a calendar..29
    4. Decide what percentage you would like to pay 29
    5. Set up automated payments whenever possible.....................30
    6. Devise a system for manual payments 31
    7. Sign up for reminders 32

What Is Revolving Credit 33
    How Does Revolving Credit Affect Your Credit Score? 33
    Payment History..34
    Amounts Owed..34
    What Does Length of Credit History Mean? 34
    What Is a Credit Mix? 37
    What is included in your Credit Mix? 37
    THE SNOWBALL EFFECT 38
    Validation Letter sent to: Budget Control Services, Inc. 43
    Remove unauthorized inquiry(ies) 45

Attorney Written Collection Letters (Step by step user guide) 47
    1. Send the collection agency proof of debt to every collection company
....47
    2. Send the XDeletion letter to the credit bureaus.......................48
    3. Send the Intent to file a lawsuit to the credit bureaus 48
    4. HIPPA Medical dispute letter:..49

Why Credit is so Important

Credit is very important because it shows creditability which is very important when you don't have cash. My story is no different than anyone else that comes from a poor upbringing. When I use the term poor, I am referring to the fact that we never had any asset or protection from any calamities that would happen in the future. Growing up, I went to the store with my parents, and they would get things from the store owner on credit until they got paid. This is a form of credit or creditability. I never knew credit was so important until my wife and I sold our house before the 2008 housing downturn. My wife and I needed a new place to live, so we needed to qualify for a new home loan, but we never monitored our credit. Unfortunately, we didn't have the knowledge, and we spent all the money that we profited off of the sale of our property. This was the greatest disaster that I've ever seen in my life. I had positioned my family to be destroyed by small hits that life would throw at us. My heart was broken for about 10 years. Thank God that my wife's parents took us in because we were homeless. We couldn't even get an apartment after we just lived in a home for 5 years. From that moment, I swore to myself that I would learn everything about credit and finance that I could. Now that I told my story, let's get into some principles of using your creditability or your ability to repay strategies that help me get my financial house in order.

The first thing we will discuss is what is a personal loan or line of credit. The personal loan or line of credit is an extension of credit in the form of cash credit or product credit. Cash credit lines can be issued by various credit card companies such as MasterCard, Visa, and American Express just to name a few. Most of society is familiar with these cards through constant marketing of goods or services through television ads or commercials. Store credit is when you use your credit to buy store items in a particular store. Take Walmart for example, they have a store card that can only be used in Walmart. Walmart also has a cash credit card that can be used in any store. Your store credit card can allow you to buy your groceries, clothing, or anything that Walmart offers through their credit card. You can buy things even without a contribution of your own cash. However, a good rule of thumb is to have the cash before you purchase most of your items so that you can pay them off quickly.

Ways to create and Improve Personal Credit with Tools of Engagement

The following eight steps are a comprehensive guide to help improve your score, but they're recognized by many experts to be the foremost important steps in building your personal credit. Take them to heart when reviewing your credit score and credit-use habits.

1. **Employ a credit reporting service.** One thing that is very important is to sign up for a monitoring service so that you can watch your score build over time. Signing up with a credit reporting service is often vital for repairing your credit and receiving fraud alerts. The corporate will offer you constant updates regarding your credit and permit you to tug regular credit reports to watch any activity on your credit profile. It's going even to provide services to get rid of negative items from your credit. However, it's essential to try to do your research and use a reputable, affordable company with a

proven diary. Historically, this industry has been worried about scam artists and frauds.

2. **Understand credit reporting.** Annualcreditreport.com is a place that you can order your credit reports from Equifax, Experian, and Transunion for FREE. Everyone has a right to one free copy per year. This tool should be used to see if there is anything on your credit report before applying for credit. You are responsible for your score and not the credit bureaus, so you have to make sure your score is right at all times. Once you receive your credit reports, look through it to see if there are any name misspellings or wrong addresses. Take the time to know how your credit score is decided, so you'll implement the right strategy. This is very important when building credit or restoring credit.

3. **Manage your payments.** Do not be 30 days or more late on any payments. Although being but 30 days late may cost you late fees and better interest rates, it won't affect your credit score drastically. Always make sure you pay your credit cards early. Use your STATEMENT DATE instead of your DUE DATE. If you use the statement date, your bills will always be paid early. This is called prepaying your credit cards. Also, you can set up Autopay, so it automatically comes out of your paycheck or bank account on a specific date. There are

financial ramifications for being late. If you are 30 days late, it can affect your credit score for up to nine months. Paying 60 days late can influence your score for up to 3 years, and being 90 days late can damage your credit for up to seven years. We would like to avoid lateness by all cost because lateness is laziness that cost us money for not paying attention to our money. We should always monitor our credit because credit can be used just like cash, so we want to stay aware of how we use our credit.

4. **How to optimize what is utilized.** Utilization ratios are vital to credit reporting agencies. "Utilization" refers to what proportion of the available credit a consumer is using on a credit card. Using 50 percent of your available credit on a card can negatively impact your credit score. Mainstream media gurus usually say that using 30 percent of your available credit can increase your credit score. That may be true if you're dropping down from 80 percent or higher. However, the best practice is to keep your total utilization under 10 percent for optimized scoring in this area. This is one of the most critical areas in your credit report. Say for example, you have 1000 dollars in total credit. This is the total when you add up all your credit cards across the board. You would only be able to spend 100 dollars or lower, which is 10 percent of your utilization. This is the amount you can spend across all of your

credit cards. I call this a VANTAGE POINT. Many experts caution consumers to never use a large percent of the available credit on any particular card. This is often considered equivalent to maxing out the card, which can negatively impact your score. I suggest you keep your score under 10 percent so that you don't owe a ton of debt. At the same time, you can build credit to pay for things that already need to be paid, such as phone bills, light or gas bills.

5. **Keep your accounts open and use them.** Whenever possible, don't close cards or accounts. An older credit card features a very positive impact on your credit score. Reporting agencies just report your information to credit card companies. Agencies will typically calculate the typical age of accounts, which may significantly impact your credit score. Moreover, it is vital to regularly use the accounts even minimally. To stop using the credit card could cause the credit issue to close the card. Just by not using the card enough could ruin your credit history in the future. You do not want to start your credit history over after it has been established. I recommend using credit building companies such as (www.self.inc) previously known as Self Lender. This company can help you build credit by using your own capital to secure a loan. You will also build or reestablish your credit by paying yourself back with a (self lender loan). I recommend using this loan for about a year to

establish your credit. You will also build up a saving from this loan and collect interest at the end of your repayment plan. However, it all depends on what you need to do to show good behavior on a ruined credit profile. Self will also help your credit overall credit mix. This account will report to all three credit bureaus. I think this is good for a rebuilding loan. This will also establish an installment loan in your credit profile. (www.capitalone.com) is another secure credit card that is pretty good for establishing revolving lines of credit into your profile. To get this established, you will need to secure the loan with a small deposit. I recommend this card to reestablish or build credit.

6. **Use good sorts of credit.** Making prompt payments on a mortgage or auto loans shows firmness and good payment history with quality loans or lines of credit. I recommend getting top tier credit cards. Building your credit gradually will take time, however, you will gain the benefit of lower interest rates. If you wait to build a strong profile, you will have a strong enough profile to get any card you desire. Therefore experts generally recommend you stand back from emporium cards due to their higher interest rates. Moreover, these sorts of credit cards aren't related to wealth- or asset-building, but rather consumer debt, detracting from your credit score instead of building it.

7. **Minimize new credit inquiries.** Most people only apply for credit when they really need it. Always use a credit building strategy when applying for credit. At the beginning of your credit building process, you can manage how many inquiries you get over time. Some of the cards that you apply for might be soft inquiries. This inquiry will not appear on your credit report. I generally advise my clients to use some soft inquiries to manage how many hard inquiries they get in a 24 month period. Every 24 months, inquiries fall off your credit report. I recommend turning down point-of-purchase credit card offers. Too many of those sorts of cards will have a negative impact on your credit rating. All the categories in your credit rating are very important, however, too much in any category without proper management can cause your score to go down. If you get 5 inquiries, Chase Bank will deny you credit; this is called the 5/24 rule. Therefore you have to be aware of how many inquiries you receive in 24 months. Management of credit inquiries makes a big difference in how many credit cards that you are able to get, so take cognizant of how many credit cards you apply for in a calendar year.

8. **Commingling spouses' credit or Piggybacking.** Piggybacking on someone's credit helps to build your credit profile. Adding an authorized user to an account is very good if he/she is someone who has great credit behavior. That great

behavior will help your credit drastically. Using a spouse or relative when mixing your personal credit can help both parties build areas in their credit profile. It'll expedite other steps down the road to have your spouse's credit linked. For instance, one spouse's credit rating may have exponential growth; this might help the person that's piggybacking to establish more creditability on their profile. The profile of the person that you use can help you establish credit quickly. Piggybacking allows you to use someone's profile to establish credit. The general plan is to establish your own primary accounts and also to help the other person or persons at the same time. By using each of your credit scores separately, you'll acquire more loans without exposure to both of your credit scores. Finally, if there is a problem with a loan down the road, the creditor can only follow the individual spouse who guaranteed the loan, not both of you. Piggybacking is a great strategy to use as long as you have a plan. If you fail to plan, then you plan to fail.

What is Annual Fee?

Annual fees are something I always look for when opening a credit card. Before I even open the card, I make sure the cards do not have any fees. Fees can stack up, especially when you have multiple cards. Always know the due date of your annual fees. You don't want to make a late payment on your credit card because you aren't aware of fees. Although I hate annual fees, there are some cards that I have applied for that had small fees. I secured a card with Wells Fargo business that had a 25 dollar fee, however, I was trying to get credit on the business credit. Sometimes fees can be beneficial as long as it is not ridiculous. If you are trying to get in the game, some small fees are actually required.

Six ways to lower your Credit Card Balances

There are multiple ways to lower your balance on available credit. This will assist you in improving your credit utilization at the same time. We will discuss six ways to pay down Debt. Our goal is to have the least amount of used credit as we can without getting the cards closed.

Pay down your balance early.
Decrease your spending.
Pay off your credit card balances with a private loan.
Increase your credit limit.
Open a replacement credit card.
Don't close unused cards.

1. Pay down your balance early.

One tricky point about credit card balance is that it affects your utilization. Credit balance and on time payments are very important when it comes to building your credit. The creditor watches how you pay off credit card balances. This behavior shows the bank how much money they are able to make off of each transaction. These transactions accumulate over time so that the bank is able to see patterns of certain behavior. Building credit has a psychological component that most people don't understand. Once the bank or credit bureaus have enough information established, they will give you a score. Everyone already have a score; however, they don't use their time to establish that score. Most people don't even pay attention to their credit until they drastically need it. Every score is associated with a rate. That rate is multiplied by your usage, so your rate is very important. Your usage depends on the balance that your card issuer reports to the credit bureaus, not what proportion you spend monthly. Those two numbers aren't always equivalent.

However, some issuers may send the info at an established time monthly for all cardholders, no matter when you're billing cycle ends. Your best bet could also be to ask your issuer so you'll be confident.

This suggests that your issuer may report your billing cycle's balance before you pay it off. This reported balance will increase or decrease your credit utilization.

However, if you pay down part or all of your balance before the statement date, your bill will go down. Make sure you know your statement date

2. Decrease your spending.

If you're working to pay down credit card debts and can't afford to form partial or full payments early, it can help to stop using your credit cards for a while. Otherwise, your new purchases may offset your payments, and your credit-utilization rate won't go down.

Switch to an open-end credit or cash for your regular purchases, and as you create credit card payments to pay off debt, your credit utilization rate will drop.

3. Pay off your credit card balances with a private loan.

Because credit utilization rates are a mirrored image of how you employ open-end credit, you'll remove a private loan, pay off your credit cards and effectively move the debt to an installment credit (potentially with a lower rate of interest than your credit cards).

However, there are multiple drawbacks to the current approach. You will need to qualify for the loan and pay a fee on the cash you borrow.

And to qualify for the most specific interest rates on a private loan, you would like to possess excellent credit (in addition to other factors). If you've got average or poor credit, the private loan's interest rate could also be higher or less than that on your credit card(s). Although this is an option, I only recommend doing this under drastic measures. It has to be a real hardship in order for me to employ this tactic.

4. Increase your credit limit.

Another way to enhance your credit utilization rate is to extend your credit limit.

You can call your credit card's issuer to request a credit limit increase; otherwise, you could also be ready to make the request online. Your card's issuer may have criteria you would like to satisfy, like having your account for a selected period of your time.

The lender will likely also base its resolution on your usage and payment history with the cardboard, so if you've got an account late payments, you're unlikely to be approved for a limit increase.

5. Open a replacement Credit Card.

Another way to extend your available credit is to open a replacement credit card.

You won't necessarily know what the credit limitation is going to be until after you're approved because it depends on the issuer's consideration of multiple factors, like your income and credit history. Some cards may have a minimum credit limitation. This is called your exposer limit. Your exposer limit is when the bank looks at your cash flow to determine how much credit they can offer. The bank tries to look at any information you have available so that they can see how much risk they can take. We are actually investments to the bank. So beware of how much you take from the banks without studying the banks.

As with requesting a credit limit increase applying for an additional card generally leads to a strict inquiry regardless if the issuer approves your application. However, once you get certain cards, you can get increases from your creditors without a hard inquiry. I employ this strategy after I have received my credit card to avoid hard inquiries

6. Don't close unused cards.

As you're taking steps to urge your credit, you'll want to filter out financial clutter by closing credit cards you do not often use.

While this might make managing your wallet easier, closing an account can lower your total available credit and decrease your credit utilization rate. So make sure you don't close out older cards with an established history. I don't recommend closing credit cards, but some credit cards have too many fees and are flat out garbage cards.

What Is a Credit-Builder Loan?

A credit-builder loan is meant to assist people that have little or no credit history build credit. An honest score makes approval for credit cards and loans at better rates more likely. Self lender is a great way to build credit if you don't have an established credit history. I've referred self lender to many of the people that I have helped to build a credit profile. This is just one of the many ways that you can get a credit builder loan. CREDIT STRONG is another lender that I recommend to build credit for people that are new to the credit game. www.creditstrong.com

How to manage a credit-builder loan

Pick the proper sort of credit-builder loan. Search for one with a payment that you can comfortably afford. Extend your budget will only raise your risk of missing a payment and damaging your score. NerdWallet approves choosing a manageable loan amount and a term not than 24 months. Choose a loan that describes payments to all or any three major credit bureaus.

Make payments on time, whenever. If you pay the loan as scheduled, you will build up good information on your credit reports. But a remittance quite 30 days late also will continue your reports and may seriously hurt your score.

Monitor your credit score. Use a private finance website like NerdWallet to urge a free credit score. NerdWallet updates your score weekly; watch your score's overall trend, but don't obsess over tiny movements.

Decide what to try to do together with your loan proceeds, plus any interest. You get the cash at the top of the loan term and, indeed, a far better credit score. If possible, use that cash as an emergency fund. Having even a couple of hundred dollars saved can insulate you from unexpected expenses that otherwise might cause debt or missed payments and score damage.

How does a credit builder loan work

Credit-builder loans pass many names, like "Fresh Start Loans" or "Starting Over Loans." they are not widely advertised and are generally offered by smaller financial institutions, like credit unions and community banks.

If you're approved for the loan, the quantity you borrow is held during a checking account while you create payments. You sometimes can't access the cash until you've got fully repaid the loan. This acts as a security net for the lender taking over risk if you've got bad credit or no credit.

Your loan payments are reported to a minimum of one agency. That helps assemble credit as long as you pay on time.

Keeping up with your credit builder loan payments is important because credit scoring models pay the utmost attention to your credit reports' payment information.

How to Apply for a Credit Card

1. Realize credit scores

Most prize credit cards require good or excellent credit. So if you have struggled to take care of honest credit history, you would possibly want to delay applying until your credit improves. Or, rather than rewards cards, you'll consider secured cards or cards designed for people with bad credit.

2. Access your credit scores

I recommend using MyFICO.com as a monitoring service, but if you have already got a credit card account, you'll also have already got access to free FICO scores on your monthly statement or online account. You can also find out if an issuer of credit cards offers a free FICO score to credit card holders. Some banks, such as Well Fargo or Navy Federal give you your actual FICO score, but they only issue one score. So you will have to find out your credit score when applying for credit. Some people use free monitoring services such as Credit Karma, Credit Sesame, or Credit IQ, which is not the very best but helps you as a guide. However, your score may not be as accurate as MYFICO. The monitoring service that you use is very important when trying to apply for credit. You might be points short of what the credit issuer is looking for. So make sure the monitoring service is pretty close to your real score as possible.

3. Improve your credit

Your credit scores will rise if you:
- Make payments on time.
- Keep balances low on existing credit cards.
- Avoid new debt.

A credit score is decided by what proportion you owe. High credit card balances are often especially damaging. Your credit utilization ratio is divided by your credit limit. You should be below 30% on each credit card. For instance, if you've got a credit limit of $10,000, it's recommended to keep the balance below $3,000. As we discussed earlier, 10% and under is the number I recommend.

Lower your credit utilization by creating a plan to pay down an existing balance as quickly as possible. And consider paying off purchases once a month to keep your balance lower throughout the month. So for example to that same example $10,000 x 1% =$100. If you use 1% of your utilization, you will be in an optimized position to keep your debt low.

4. Don't apply for credit until you understand it

You may not get approved for a card with a huge sign-up bonus and lucrative rewards if you've got bad credit. Each credit card application can temporarily ding your credit report, so think about using a web tool to pre-qualify.

You can also call the card issuer and ask a few specific card requirements. You'll have an easier time getting approved for a secured credit card, which uses a cash deposit you create upon approval to "secure" your line of credit. A number of the best-secured cards offer cash rewards, flexible deposit amounts, and, therefore, the chance to upgrade to an unsecured card (and get your deposit back).

5. Include all income within the application

Issuers consider your credit scores an indicator of creditworthiness, but scores don't reflect your income. Card issuers use the revenue to calculate your debt-to-income ratio, which helps determine your ability to pay. Change your ratio by either increasing revenue or decreasing debt.

A PRIMARY CARD HOLDER VS. AUTHORIZED USER

What is a primary card holder?

An authorized user is a cardholder on someone else's credit card account. You've got a credit card in your name that's linked to the first cardholder's account. The person who initially applied for the credit card is the primary credit card holder.

How to become an authorized user.

The primary cardholder has got to add you as an authorized user. You'll either use online via your bank's mobile app or over the phone. The method is often completed within a couple of minutes, and your card will likely be mailed to the first cardholder's address. Sometimes there's the choice to ship the cardboard to an alternate address.

And if you already added someone as authorized users on one card from an issuer, the method is usually quicker to feature them to another card from an equivalent issuer. For instance, if you already added your spouse to your Blue Cash Preferred Card from American Express, you'd just need to select their name to feature them on your American Express Gold Card. Piggybacking is a good thing, however, it should not be looked at the same as your primary accounts. You also want to make sure that you are building your own primary accounts for optimal credit scoring. So although I recommend using authorized users, you still should be building your own primary credit cards simultaneously.

How to use a Personal Loan to create credit

A personal loan may help with most of the five factors that influence your credit scores. Payment history: Getting a loan and making all of your monthly payments on time establishes a diary of responsibility. This is often a primary thing about building a positive credit profile.

Credit usage: What proportion of debt you've got and what kind reflects how well you manage credit. Having a private loan can help with this, as long as you pay it back consistent with the terms and do not compile an excessive amount of other debt.

Length of credit history: A more extended credit history can show you being responsible with credit over time, strengthening your credit profile. If you've never used credit, getting a private loan can assist you in starting this process.

Credit mix and types: If your credit history is restricted, having varying sorts of credit, like credit cards, personal loans, and mortgages, can boost your credit scores.

Why you ought to consider before employing a consumer loan to create credit

Using a consumer loan responsibly may assist you in building credit, but it's going to not be the simplest option for everybody, and there are ways in which a private loan also can hurt your credit.

Late payments will hurt your credit.

As with any sort of credit, one obvious risk with personal loans is that payments 30 days late or more typically show abreast of your credit reports which can lower your credit scores.

Bad-credit and no-credit personal loans are expensive.

Having less-than-stellar credit might not stop you from getting approved with certain lenders, but there's usually a price to pay when you're considered a higher-risk borrower. Some personal loans accompany an annual percentage rate of quite 30%, while fees related to payday loans translate to triple-digit APRs.

APRs can include both interest and costs, so it is vital to read the fine print to understand what you're paying for.

Short-term loans are often dangerous.

While some personal loans offer you years to pay back what you owe, some small loans, including payday loans, may offer you as little as every week or two and need one payment.

If you cannot afford to pay the loan back in time, you'll be forced to renew it or remove another one to form the payment, which may throw you into a vicious circle of debt.

Not all personal lenders report back to the main credit bureaus.

Are you trying to use a private loan to create credit? Imagine checking out that your activity isn't reported to any of the three major credit line bureaus.

Unfortunately, that is the case with some personal loans. If you are not careful, you'll spend months or maybe years making on-time payments without it being reflected on your credit reports.

How to Report Rent Payments to an agency

Rent payments aren't always included in credit scores because they're not routinely reported to credit bureaus. However, rent is the most considerable monthly expense for several people. Approximately 25% of renters spend quite half their income on rent, and nearly 50% spend quite 30% of their income on rent. There are some options for reporting rent payments to the credit agency.

a. Check with Your Landlord

Your landlord already may report rent payments to the credit bureaus employing a service that handles the method. Timely rent payments will help improve your credit score if your landlord says them, but late payments can have a negative impact on your score.

b. Use credit cards to pay your rent.

While your rent payments won't be listed as a different trade line on your credit report, using your credit card for your rent can still boost your credit score. Check to see whether your landlord accepts credit card payments and note any service fees which may be charged for employing a credit card. If you're employing a rewards credit card to pay your rent, you'll earn points or cash back on your rent payments.

When you use a credit card to pay your rent, confirm to pay off your full balance, even if you were paying rent. That is the best thanks to staying out of debt, improving your credit score, and obtaining the complete advantage of making timely rent payments.

c. Use a Rent Reporting Service

Several companies will report rent payments on your behalf. Monthly fees vary between services, and a few charge an initial enrollment fee to urge started. In some cases, your landlord may need to confirm your rent payments for them to be included in your credit report. Note that even when rent payments are included in your credit report, they'll not be included in your credit score calculation.

1. Rental Kharma will add up to 6 months of past rent payments to your credit report. The registration fee is $50 per person, and therefore the monthly charge is $8.95 as of March 2020. Your entire rental history is often added for a fee of $30 or $60, counting on how long you have been at your current address. Rental Kharma reports to TransUnion.

2. Rent Reporters features a sign-up fee of $94.95 and charges $9.95 for monthly agency reporting as of March 2020. Once you check-in, Rent Reporters verifies your rental history together with your landlord, then reports the trade line to the credit bureaus. The service includes a replica of your credit score. Rent Reporters reports to TransUnion.

3. Rock the score verifies your rent payments with your landlord's monthly updates to your credit score with your payment information. You'll pay $25 to enroll in the service and $8.95 monthly for ongoing reporting as of March 2020.

There's also a choice to add 24 months of rental payment history to your credit report. Rock the Score reports to TransUnion

d. Making Rent Payments

If you enroll during a rent reporting service, confirm you understand whether you'll still pay your rent to your landlord or whether you'll make payments to the service provider.

Pay your rent on time monthly, even when it isn't reported to the credit bureaus. Late payments can cause an eviction that would ultimately land on your credit report through a set of judgments. At that time, the late rent payments hurt your credit score instead of helping it.

How to make timely payments on all of your bills

This Seven tips to assist you to pay your bills on time

1. Make an inventory of each bill

It's almost impossible to pay all of your accounts on time if you do not know all of your obligations, so identifying your creditors, vendors, and repair providers is often a superb place to start out.

If you've got tons of bills to pay, some can fall through the cracks. To avoid this, check your credit reports and list every lender (leave out paid off). Next, review recent bank and credit card statements to feature any recurring obligations to your list. This might include gym memberships, cell phone bills, media subscriptions, online services (like music or other apps), and utility bills.

Your list should include the lender or service provider, the minimum monthly payment, and, therefore, the total balance due. Once you have your list, consider separating bills into two categories: people who are often paid automatically and people that can't.

2. Determine when your payments are due

Once you have got an inventory of bills to pay, determine when each account is due and add it to your list. If your due dates are all over the place, you'll want to tweak them to form tracking payments easier.

Many creditors allow you to select or change the date you pay, so go browsing or call to seek out.

3. Add your payments to a calendar

Tracking your bills' due dates through a calendar or other system can be a good idea for monitoring input and output of debt.

For example, if you employ a web calendar, you'll add payments there. It's always easy to feature recurring events, and your calendar app may have handy tools (like color coding), so due dates stand out from other events.

4. Decide what percentage you would like to pay

For some of your bills, you'll need to pay a group amount. Others, including credit cards, may allow you to spend the maximum amount or as little as you would like after making the minimum monthly payment.

Ideally, you'd pay the complete balance due on all of your bills every billing cycle, even on the credit cards and other accounts that allow you to hold a monthly balance. This might not always be possible. Except for accounts that will enable you to take care of a balance, you'll plan to pay quite the minimum to assist you to save on interest, avoid build-up unnecessary debt, or potentially become debt-free faster.

While changes may take a few billing cycles to go into effect, having the same due date for multiple bills can simplify your life. And it can be helpful to set up your bills for right after payday if you're concerned about overspending and not having enough money left to pay them later.

5. Set up automated payments whenever possible

Armed with your list and your calendar, it's time to set up your payment system. One approach is to pay as many bills as possible automatically.

When you set up automated payments through creditors, you can specify whether you want them to debit the minimum due, the full balance due, or another amount (if the accounts allow it).

While many lenders accept automated payments from bank accounts, you may also have another option for certain monthly obligations charging your regular bills to one of your credit cards.

But it's best to use a credit card to pay your monthly bills only if you're confident you can afford to pay the card on time and in full. Otherwise, you may build up a balance that will charge you interest, and that could undermine your efforts to stay on top of your bills.

6. Devise a system for manual payments

While it can be an excellent idea to autopay as much as you can, you may not be able to pay everything automatically, or you may not want to. So, for those bills, you pay manually, you can set up a separate system.

Pay your bills immediately. If you take this approach, the goal is to pay the bill right away. You can go online and make a payment as soon as your statement posts or bill arrives - or you can sit down and write the check, put it in an envelope, and drop it in the mail the next time you go out.

Pay your bills on a certain day each month. If you don't want to jump online every time you get a bill or stop what you're doing to write a check, you can set aside a regular, recurring time to pay your bills. It may help to schedule a block of time on your calendar. But even if you take a less formal approach, try to make it part of your routine.

7. Sign up for reminders

Whether you auto pay or handle bills manually, it's helpful to be reminded when bills come due.

You can remind yourself to make a payment or to check if an automatic payment is cleared.

Your calendar reminders may be enough. Another approach is to use a specialized app for organizing your money and reminding you about bills. You may also be able to sign up for alerts directly with creditors and vendors. www.Mint.com is a good way to manage all your debt in one place. This can be a great way to stay debt free.

What Is Revolving Credit

Revolving credit means you're borrowing against a line of credit. Let's say a lender extends a certain amount of credit to you, against which you can borrow repeatedly. The amount of credit you're allowed to use each month is your credit line or credit limit. You're free to use as much or as little of that credit line as you wish on any purchase you could make with cash.

At the end of each statement period, you receive a bill for the balance. If you don't pay it off in full, you carry the balance or revolve it over to the next month and pay interest on any remaining balance. As you pay down the balance, more of your credit line becomes available.

How Does Revolving Credit Affect Your Credit Score?

Any time you spend on credit can impact your FICO credit score, most commonly used by lenders. How you handle your credit will determine whether the impact is positive or negative.

Payment History

Credit bureaus consider several factors when calculating your FICO credit score. The biggest, accounting for 35% of your score, is your payment history.

Missing payments on credit cards or other revolving credit accounts can have a dramatic and lasting impact on your score. But if you consistently make your payments by the due date, you will build a positive payment history that strengthens your score over time.

Amounts Owed

The second-most-important factor in determining your FICO score is the amounts owed, which accounts for 30% of your score. Relying too heavily on credit extended to you is a major red flag to lenders since it might appear you don't have enough money to keep up with expenses. The last thing you want to do is max out your credit lines.

What Does Length of Credit History Mean?

The longer your credit history, the better it is for your credit score. That's because lenders are more comfortable with borrowers who have a long history of paying their bills on time. Customers with a short credit history haven't yet shown that they can be trusted to make their payments on time over the long haul. Having an established credit history is one way to improve your credit score.

Chief Executive Officer and Founder Jared Weitz of United Capital Source in Great Neck, New York, said that consumers with more extended credit history with no missed payments would put lenders at ease. They'll also have better credit scores, another positive factor that makes lenders more willing to loan them money for mortgages, auto loans, personal loans, or student loans.

"The longer an account has been open and active, the better it will be for helping boost your credit score," Weitz said. "Not only does this demonstrate your capacity to maintain your credit, but it also shows what your patterns are over time as a borrower."

This is one reason why Weitz recommends not closing old credit card accounts even if you pay them off and have no intention of using them again. First, this hurts your credit utilization ratio. Your credit score will improve if you're using less of your available credit. If you close a credit card account, you'll automatically lower the amount of credit you have available to you. Even if you don't add to your debt, you'll be hurting your credit utilization ratio.

Closing an account after opening a new credit card will also hurt your length of credit history. That's because you're eliminating an older, existing credit line and replacing it with a new one. That will automatically lower the average age of your credit accounts.

"Even if you decide you no longer want to spend on a certain credit card, don't close the account," Weitz said. "When you keep the account open, it helps build your credit history while also maintaining or improving your credit-utilization ratio."

CREDIT MIX

What Is a Credit Mix?

Credit mix refers to the types of accounts that make up a consumer's credit report. The credit mix determines 10% of a consumer's FICO score. The different types of credit that might be part of a consumer's credit mix include credit cards, student loans, automobile loans, and mortgages. Credit mix has a more considerable impact on a score if there is not much information in the consumer's credit file compared with having more substantial details of credit usage and repayment by the consumer.

What is included in your Credit Mix?

Credit cards (revolving)

Home equity line of credit (revolving)

Student loans (installment)

Auto loans (installment)

Mortgages (installment)

Personal loans (installment

THE SNOWBALL EFFECT

The Snowball Effect is a concept that I learned from reading Warren Buffett's book the Snowball Effect. When looking at a snowball, we notice that it builds as it rolls down a hill. We should concentrate on building our wealth by controlling our debt. Live below your means. Always save more than you spend. Be sure to build that wealth like a growing snowball.

HERE A FEW LETTERS BELOW TO HELP REMOVE INQUIRIES:

Request for VALIDATION, NOT Verification

Your Name

Your Street Address

Your City, State, and Zip Code August 29th, 2014

Company: NCO FINANCIAL SYSTEMS INC.

Address: 507 Prudential Rd.

City/ State/ Zip: Horsham, PA. 19044

RE: Account # AOR081 To Whom It May Concern:

This letter is being sent to you in response to notices sent to me from your company and more importantly, due to your erroneous reporting to the Credit Bureau{s}, the highly negative impact on my personal credit report. Please be advised that this is not a refusal to pay, but a notice sent pursuant to the Fair Debt Collection Practices Act, 15 USC 1692g Sec. 809 {b} that your claim is disputed, and validation is requested.

This is NOT a request for "verification" or proof of my mailing address, but a request for VALIDATION made pursuant to the above-named Title and Section. I respectfully request that your offices provide me with competent evidence that I have any legal obligation to pay you.

Please provide me with the following:

What the money you say I owe is for:
Explain and show me how you calculated what you say I owe:
Provide me with copies of any papers that show I agreed to pay what you say I owe:
Provide a verification or copy of any judgment if applicable:
Identify the original creditor:
Prove the Statute of Limitations has not expired on this account:
Show me that you are licensed to collect in my state:
Provide me with your license numbers and Registered Agent or Agent of Service:

At this time, I will also inform you that if your offices have reported invalidated information to any of the 3 major Credit Bureau {Experian, Equifax, or TransUnion} this action might constitute fraud under both Federal and State Laws. Due to this fact, if any negative mark is found on any of my credit reports by your company or the company that you represent, I will not hesitate to bring legal action against you for the following:

Violation of the Fair Credit Reporting Act

Violation of the Fair Debt Collection Practices Act

Defamation of Character

If your offices are able to provide proper documentation as requested in the following Declaration, I will require at least 30 days to investigate this information and during such time, all collection activity must cease.

Also, during this validation period, if any action is taken, which could be considered detrimental to any of my credit reports, I will consult with my legal counsel for a suit. This includes listing any information with a credit reporting repository that could be inaccurate or invalidated or verifying an account as accurate, when in fact, there is no provided proof that it is accurate.

If your company fails to respond to this validation request within 30 days from the date of your receipt, all references to this account must be deleted and completely removed from my credit report, and a copy of such deletion {to any/all of the 3 major credit reporting bureaus: Equifax, Experian, and TransUnion} request shall be sent to me immediately.

I would also like to request, in writing, that no telephone contact be made by your company to my home or my place of employment. If your offices attempt telephone communication with me, including but not limited to computer generated calls and calls or correspondence sent to or with any third parties, it will be considered harassment, and I will have no choice but to file suit. All future communications with me MUST be done in writing and sent to the address noted in this letter by USPS.

It would be advisable that you assure me that your records are in order before I am forced to take legal action against your company and your client. This is an attempt to correct your records, any information obtained shall be used for that purpose.

Best Regards,

Your Name

October 29th, 2020 Experian

P.O. Box 4500

Allen, TX 75013

RE: Intent to file a lawsuit, HIPPA Privacy Violation

Validation Letter sent to: Budget Control Services, Inc.

P.O. Box 370107 Denver, CO 80237

Account #528377-379535

To Whom It May Concern:

Please be advised I have requested "validation" {not verification} of an item reported to you by the above original creditor/collection agency. I have received a response that clearly violates my rights according to HIPPA.

Budget Control Services, Inc. did NOT provide me with a HIPPA release that releases my medical information to them; therefore by providing such information, they are in VIOLATION of my HIPPA rights. I am proceeding with legal action as prescribed by law against the above-named original creditor/collection agency should this item not be deleted within the required time allowed by law. I will seek every legal remedy available to me and file a suit against the credit bureau responsible for reporting this violation.

I urge you to take this extremely seriously, as I have documented my case without error. I encourage a response from you expeditiously.

Sincerely

Your Name

Your Street Address

Your City, State, and Zip Code

Remove unauthorized inquiry(ies)

[[Date]]

[[Credit Bureau Name]] [[Address]]

[[City, State, Zip]]

Dear [[Credit Bureau Name]]:

Dear [[Credit Bureau Name]]:

I am writing to you to request that you remove the following unauthorized inquiry(ies) from my credit report:

Creditor: [[Creditor Name]]

Inquiry Date: [[Date]]

Attached is a copy of the letter that I have sent directly to the creditor disputing their reporting.

I understand that per the Fair Credit Reporting Act, you are required to notify me of your investigation results within 30 days. My contact information is provided below, and I have included proof of my social security and current address to avoid any delays in your response time.

I look forward to receiving an updated copy of my credit report reflecting the above correction. Thank you in advance.

Sincerely,

[[Your Name]] [[Your Address]] [[Your SS#]l [[Your DOB]]

Attorney Written Collection Letters
(Step by Step User Guide)

When disputing items on your credit report, the first thing you need to do is obtain a copy of your credit report. The best way to accomplish this is to order a FREE one from:

http:// www.annualcreditreport.com. Every person can get a free copy of their credit report. This report will not have credit scores but will have credit information.

Once you receive your credit report, here are the steps to delete any negative entries.

1. Send the collection agency proof of debt to every collection company

   a) This is your first initial contact with the collection agency.
   b) You need delivery confirmation, save receipt or email from USPS confirming delivery.

c) Wait for a response from the collection agency. The goal is not to get one.
  d) **Full account numbers may not be provided on your credit report. You can instead cut and paste each delinquent account and include each account snapshot with the letter.

2. Send the XDeletion letter to the credit bureaus

  a) You have to send this letter to all credit bureaus that are reporting.
  b) You must send a copy of your Driver's license, SSN card, and proof of address. Use a utility bill or phone bill with your full name and address.
  c) You need delivery confirmation, save receipt or email from USPS confirming delivery.
  d) Wait for your response from the collection agency.
  e) **To include account number, if not known in full, please see asterisk above.

3. Send the Intent to file a lawsuit to the credit bureaus

  a) Send to all credit bureaus and collection agencies if response is not received within 30 days. This is a simple reminder of the Fair Credit Act laws to the credit bureaus, which forces them to delete account if validation is not received. I would send this even if I received a validation from the collection company. Sometimes collection companies send the validation to you but not to the credit bureaus.

*Repeat the process until the collection agency doesn't perform the validation within the 30 day period. This strategy works best for debt that the collection agency can't validate. Therefore, your negative item is removed.

4. HIPPA Medical dispute letter:

This letter was written with the intention of reminding the collection agencies and credit bureaus that if they fully validate your validation letter on your medical bills, they are violating HIPPA regulations. HIPPA laws do not allow your doctor or health care provider to disclose your medical information without your consent of HIPPA release. There's been a steady increase of doctors asking for a HIPPA release to be signed by you, however, this only allows them to share with other medical professionals and not 3rd party collectors. Make sure you exclude everyone other than the party intended to receive your medical information (do not sign a full HIPPA release).

This medical dispute letter should be used after the 3 letters above have been sent. Sometimes the collection agencies send your health records as validation. If they do this, include a copy of this and send it to the credit bureaus. Thereby proving they have broken HIPPA laws (a major violation of the Privacy Act laws!).

Experian

P.O. Box 4500 Allen, TX 75013

Equifax Information Services LLC

P.O. Box 740256 Atlanta, GA 30374

TransUnion LLC Consumer Dispute Center

P.O. Box 2000 Chester, PA 19022

October 16, 2020

TransUnion LLC Consumer Dispute Center

P.O. Box 2000 Chester, PA 19022

RE: Intent to file lawsuit, no response for Validation documentation.

Validation Letter sent to: Victoria's Secret

P.O. Box 182685 Columbus, OH. 43218

Account #81418

To Whom It May Concern:

Please be advised I have requested "validation" {not verification} of an item reported to you by the above original creditor/collection agency. I have received no response from them and/or no proof to validate their claim.

They have broken the law by their non-response within the time period allowed by law. I am proceeding with legal action as prescribed by law against the above-named original creditor/collection agency. Should this item not be deleted within the required time allowed by law, I will seek every legal remedy available to me and file a suit against the credit bureau responsible for reporting this erroneous claim.

I urge you to take this extremely seriously, as I have documented my case without error. I encourage a response from you expeditiously.

Sincerely
Your Name
Your Street Address
Your City, State, and Zip Code

Remove unauthorized inquiry(ies)

([Date]]
LexisNexis Consumer Center Attn; Security Freeze
P.O. Box 105108 Atlanta, GA 30348-5108

Dear [[Credit Bureau Name]]:

I am writing to you to request that you remove the following unauthorized inquiry(ies) from my credit report:

Creditor: [[Creditor Name]]
Inquiry Date: [[Date]]

Attached is a copy of the letter that I have sent directly to the creditor disputing their reporting.

I understand that per the Fair Credit Reporting Act, you are required to notify me of your investigation results within 30 days. My contact information is provided below, and I have included proof of my social security and current address to avoid any delays in your response time.

I look forward to receiving an updated copy of my credit report reflecting the above correction. Thank you in advance.

Sincerely,

[[Your Name]] [(Your Address)) [[Your SS#]]
[[Your DOB])

September 16, 2020

Equifax Information Services LLC
P.O. Box 740256 Atlanta, GA 30374

Re: Complaint Letter to Delete Inaccurate Information Dear Sir or Madam:

I respectfully request your prompt attention on the following inaccurate information on my credit report. For your convenience, the disputed item is listed on the enclosed page of my credit report.

The following item is inaccurate and negatively affecting my credit. Please reinvestigate this matter and delete and/or correct the disputed item. I respectfully request that you provide me with proof of the disputed item, specifically any contract, note, court documents, or any instrument bearing my signature. Failing that, this item must be deleted.

Item: MCT GROUP
Account# M300SDT1000546662 Reason: NOT MY ACCOUNT

It is my understanding that under law, you have 30 days from the receipt of this letter to verify this item. It should be understood that failure to do so within the 30-day period constitutes a reason to immediately delete this item from my credit report. {FCRA 15 U.SC. section 1681 (5) (A).

Also, pursuant to 15 U.S.C. section 1681i (6) (A) of the Fair Credit Reporting Act, please notify me the item has been deleted. You may send an updated copy of my credit report to the below address. According to the provisions of 15 U.S.C. section 1681j, there should be no charge for this notification.

Sincerely,
Full Name Street Address
City, State, and zip code SSN:
Date of Birth September 16, 2020
Experian
P.O. Box 4500 Allen, TX 75013

Re: Complaint Letter to Delete Inaccurate Information Dear Sir or Madam:

I respectfully request your prompt attention on the following inaccurate information on my credit report. For your convenience, the disputed item is listed on the enclosed page of my credit report.

The following item is inaccurate and negatively affecting my credit. Please reinvestigate this matter and delete and/or correct the disputed item. I respectfully request that you provide me with proof of the disputed item, specifically any contract, note, court documents, or any instrument bearing my signature. Failing that, this item must be deleted.

Item: MCT GROUP

Account# M300SDT1000546662 Reason: NOT MY ACCOUNT

It is my understanding that under law, you have 30 days from the receipt of this letter to verify this item. It should be understood that failure to do so within the 30-day period constitutes a reason to immediately delete this item from my credit report. {FCRA 15 U.SC. section 1681 (5) (A).

Also, pursuant to 15 U.S.C. section 1681i (6) (A) of the Fair Credit Reporting Act, please notify me the item has been deleted. You may send an updated copy of my credit report to the below address. According to the provisions of 15 U.S.C. section 1681j, there should be no charge for this notification.

Sincerely,

Full Name Street Address

City, State, and zip code SSN:

Date of Birth:

I would like to thank you for reading this book. Even if you never employ all of the strategies in this book. I am still thankful to give this information even if I can help just one person. Most of the concepts will be needed in your life at some point. It's good to have some kind of information that can help you out of a bad situation, I hope this book has armed you with some tools to start your credit building journey. I would love for everyone to thrive, not survive. Understanding credit is very important, and it affects all of us in some capacity. Congratulations on your first step towards a great credit building journey.

www.ingramcontent.com/pod-product-compliance
Lightning Source LLC
Chambersburg PA
CBHW050300220526
45465CB00002B/763